RAMADAN

COLORING BOOK FOR KIDS

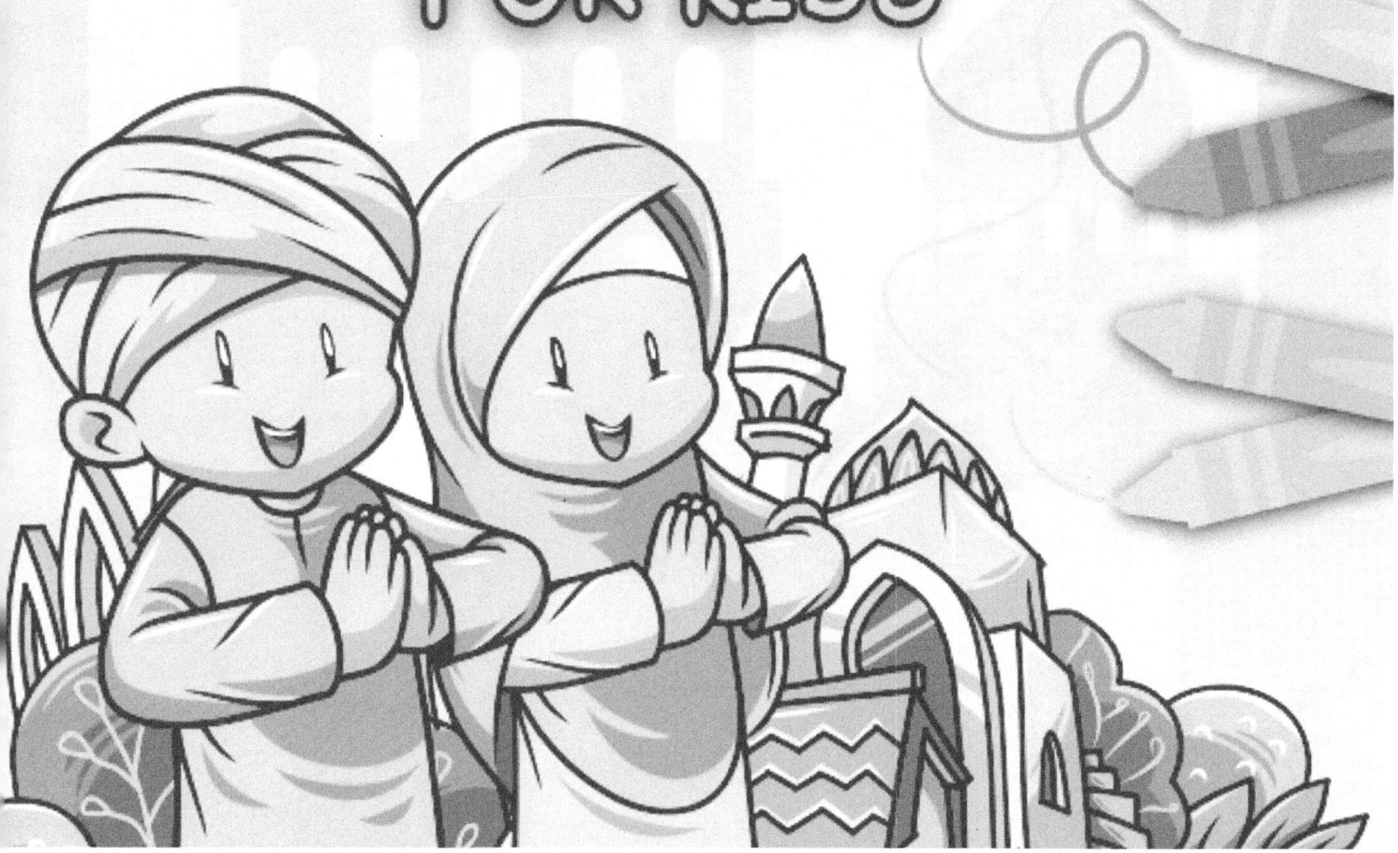

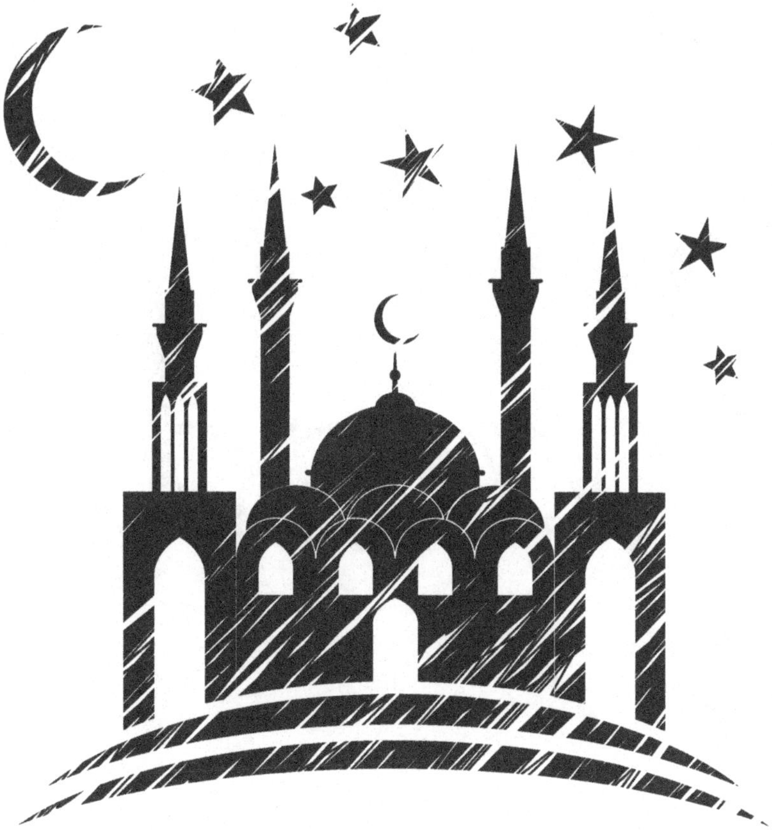

This Ramadan Coloring Book Belongs To:

Ramadan Kareem

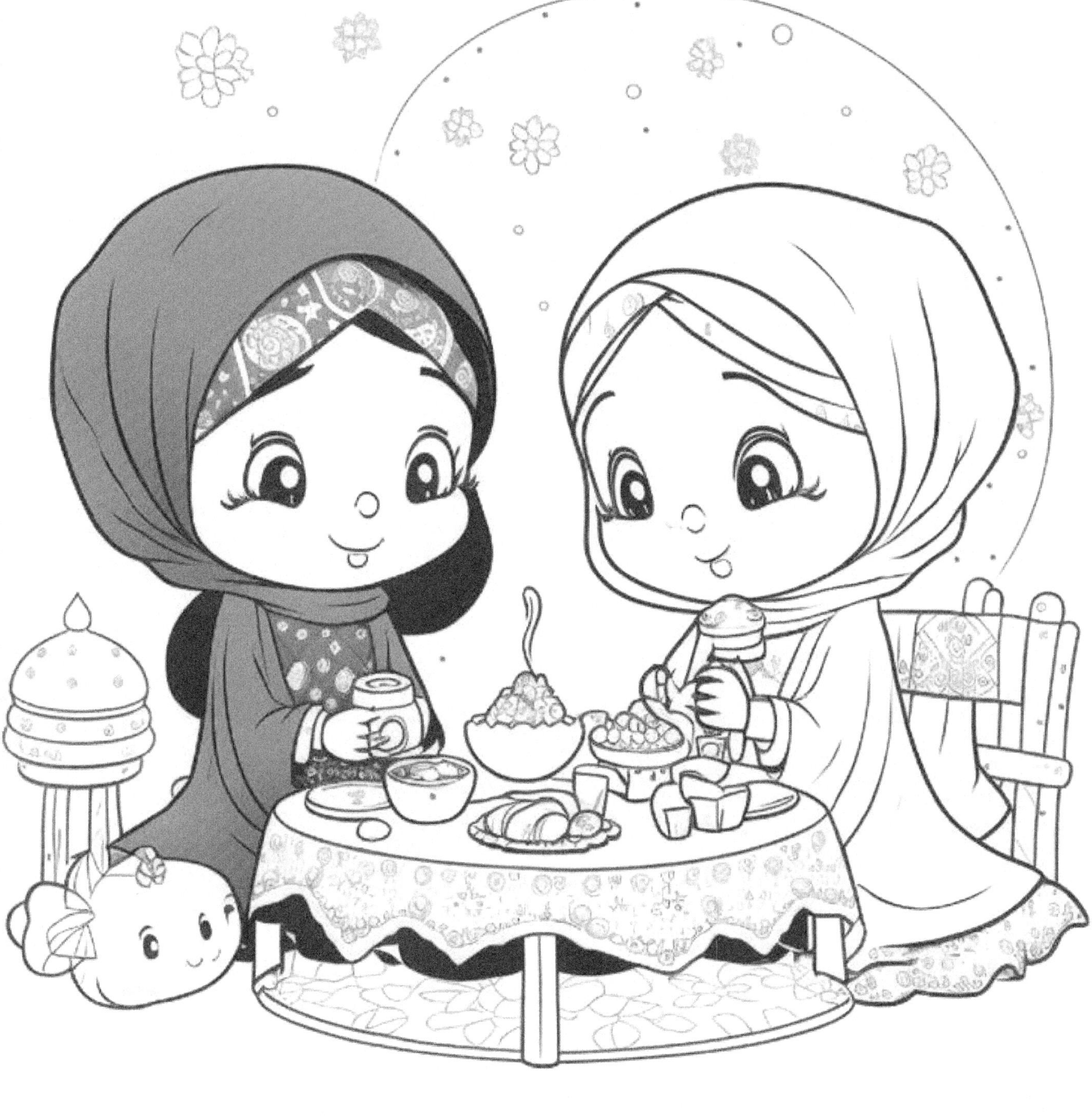

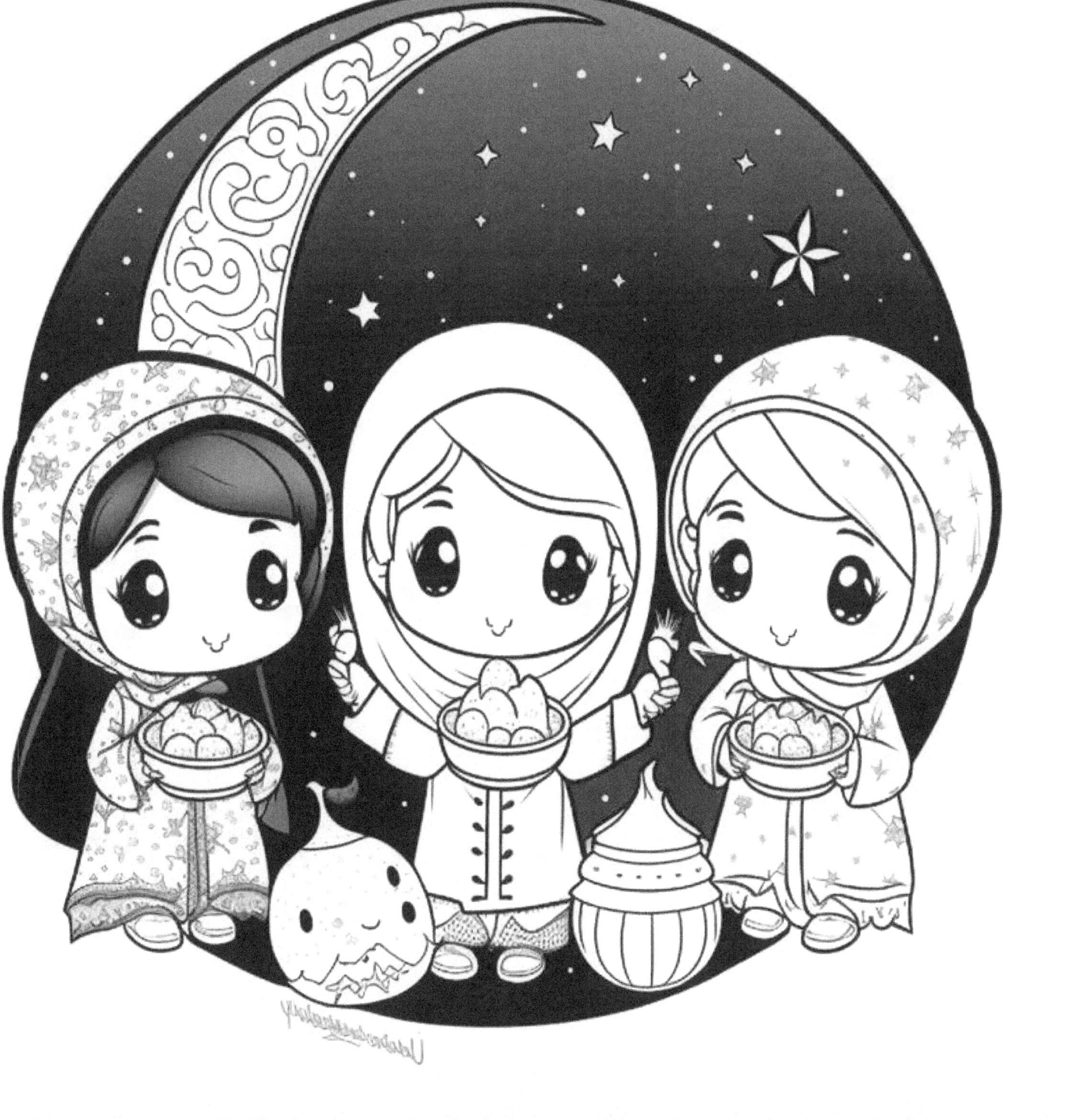

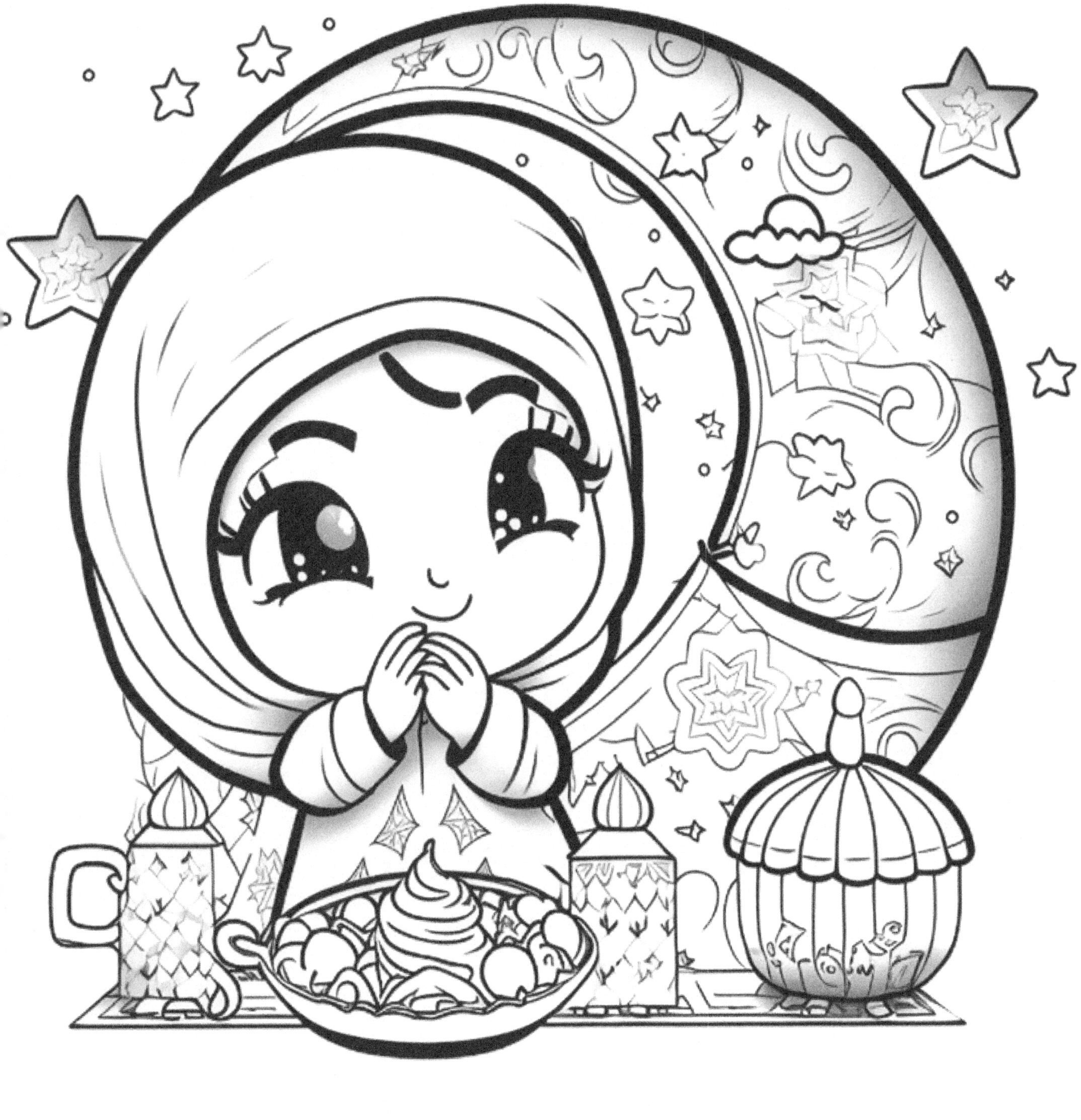

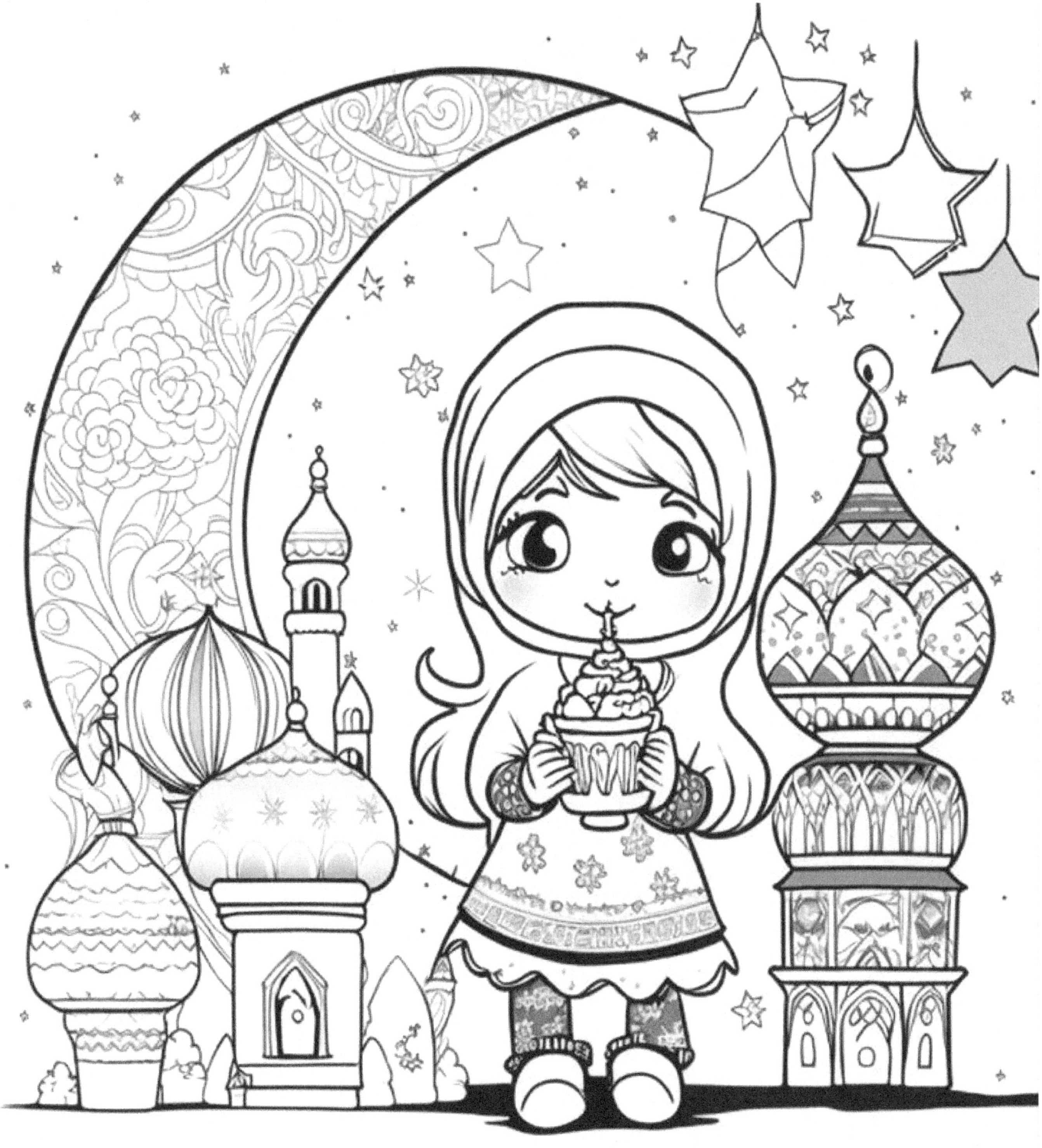

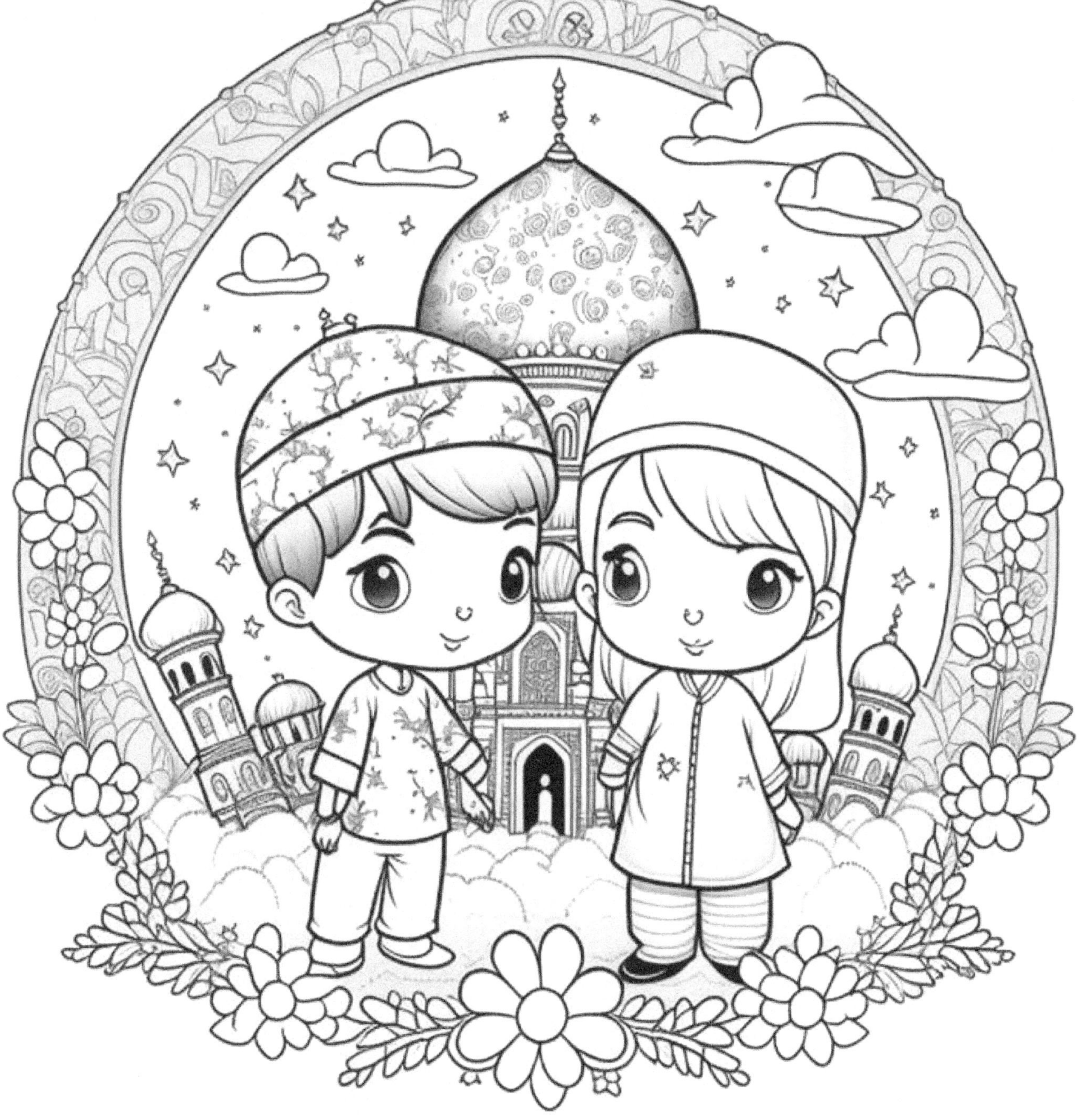

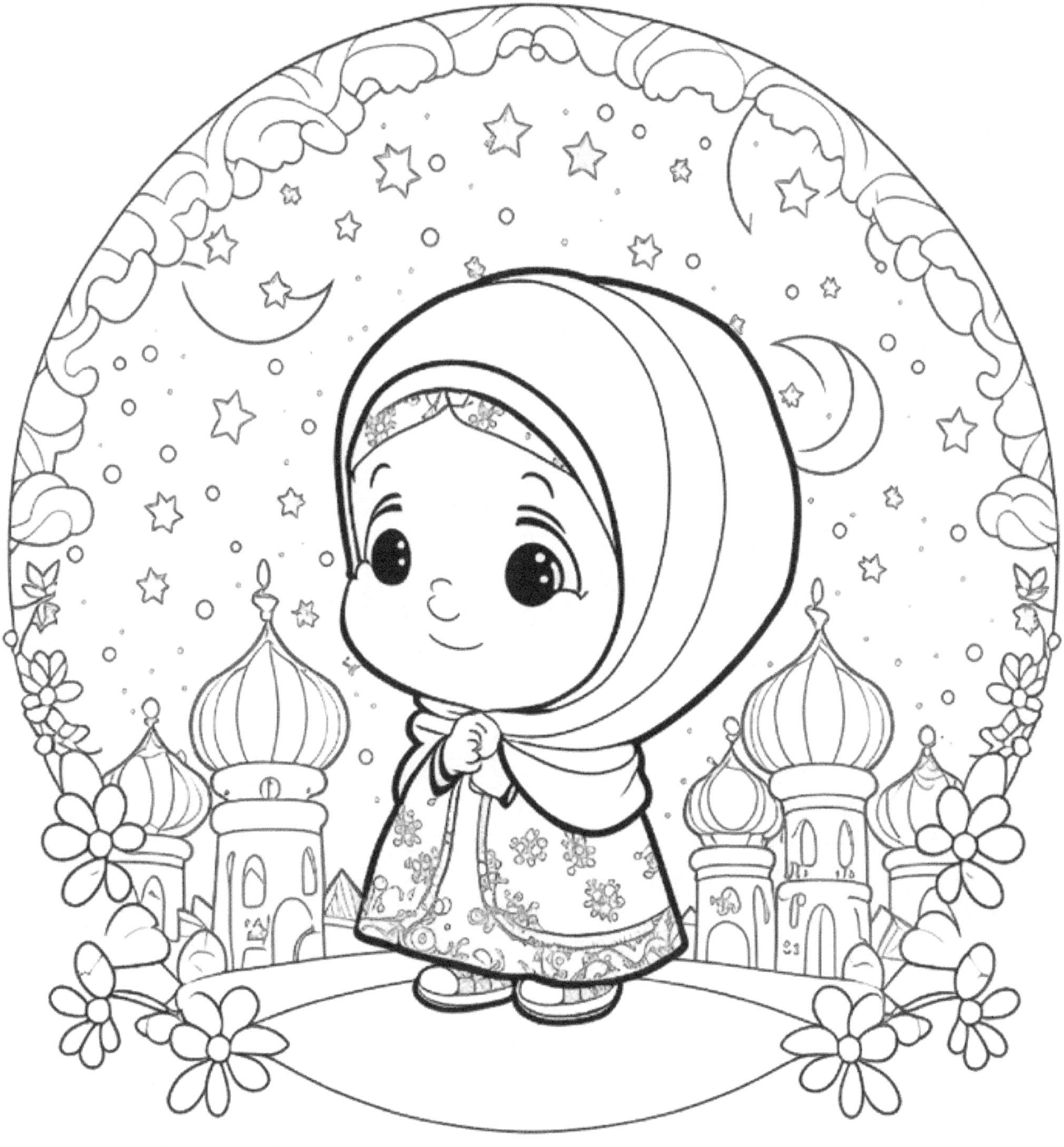

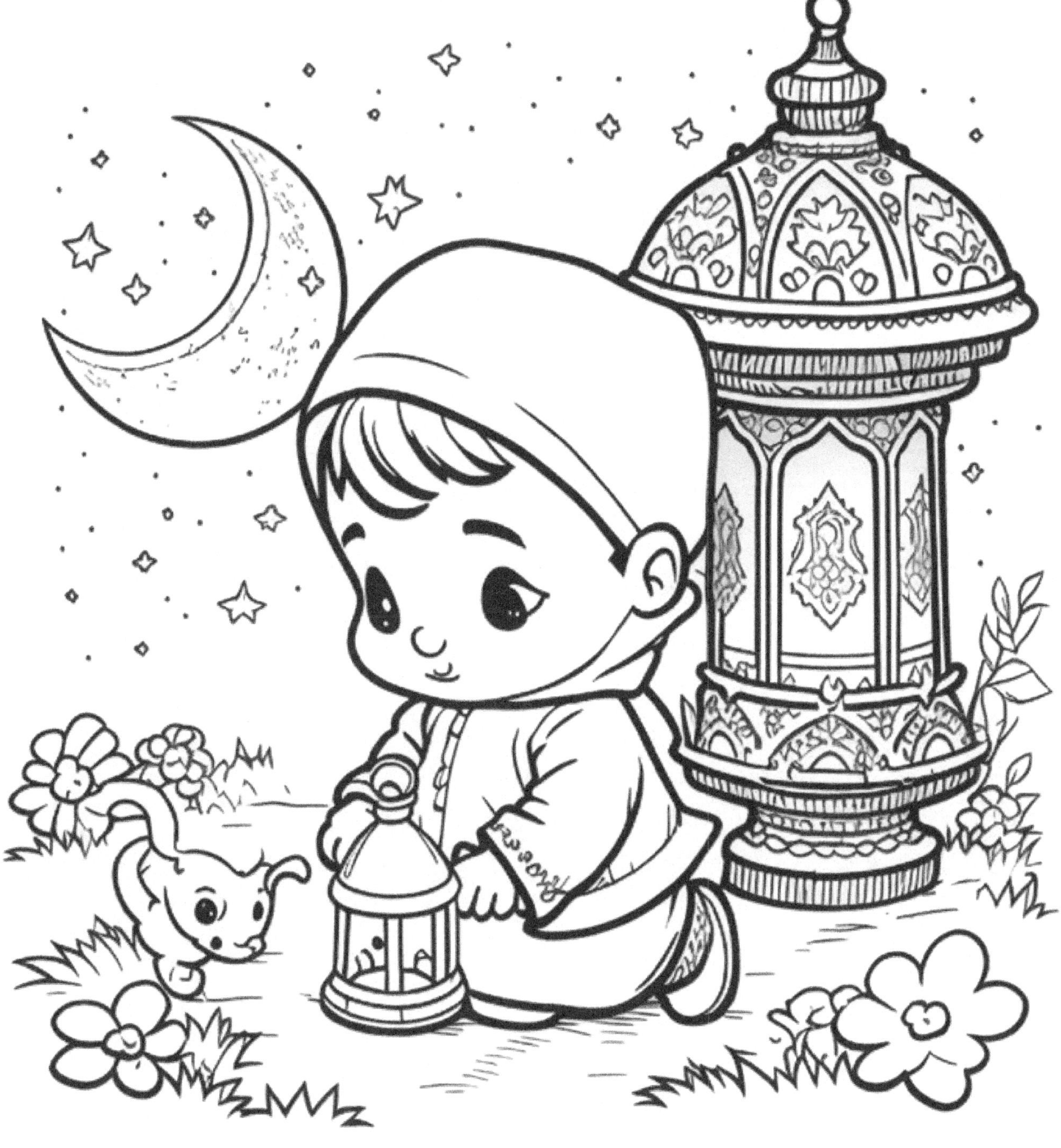

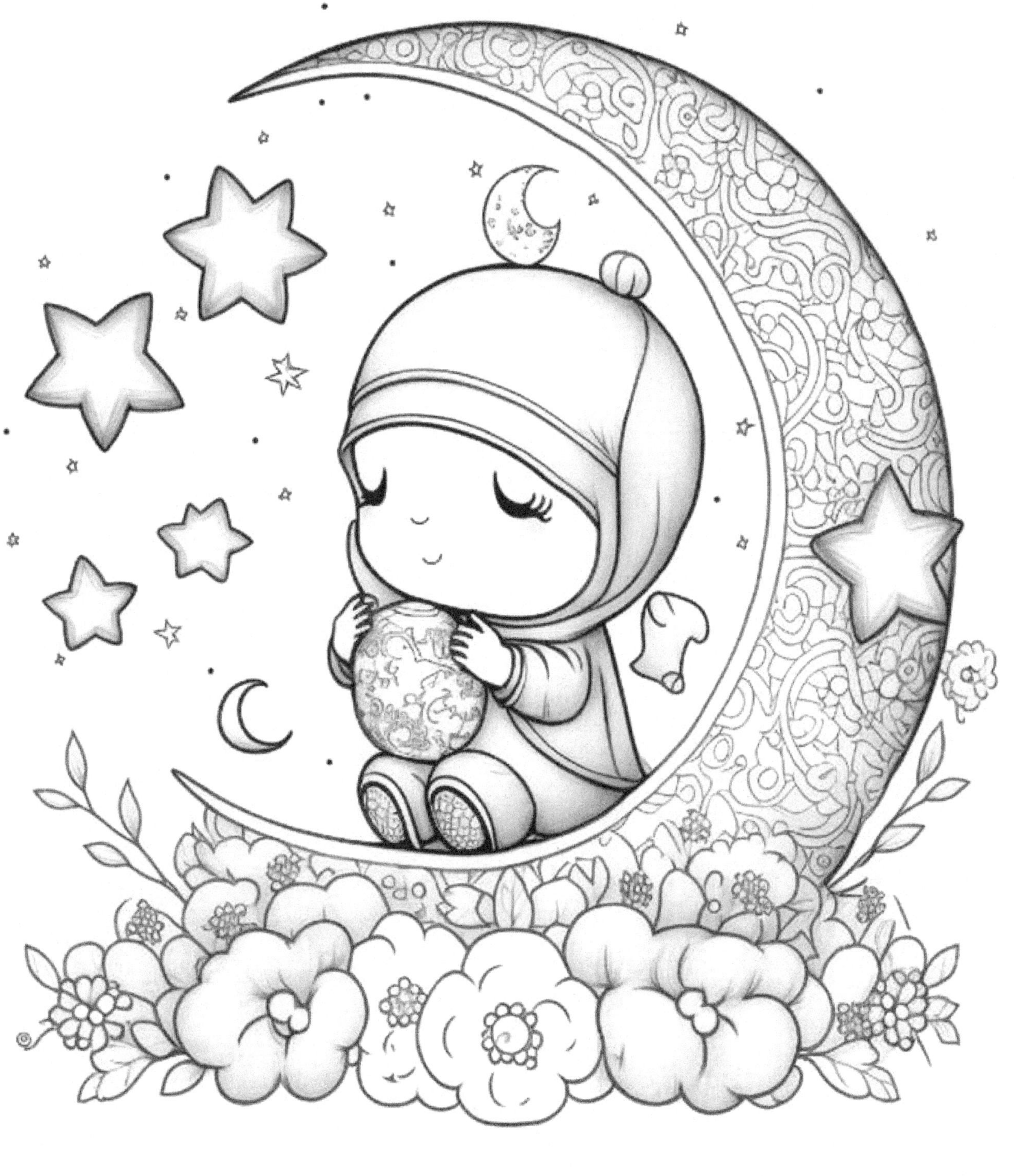

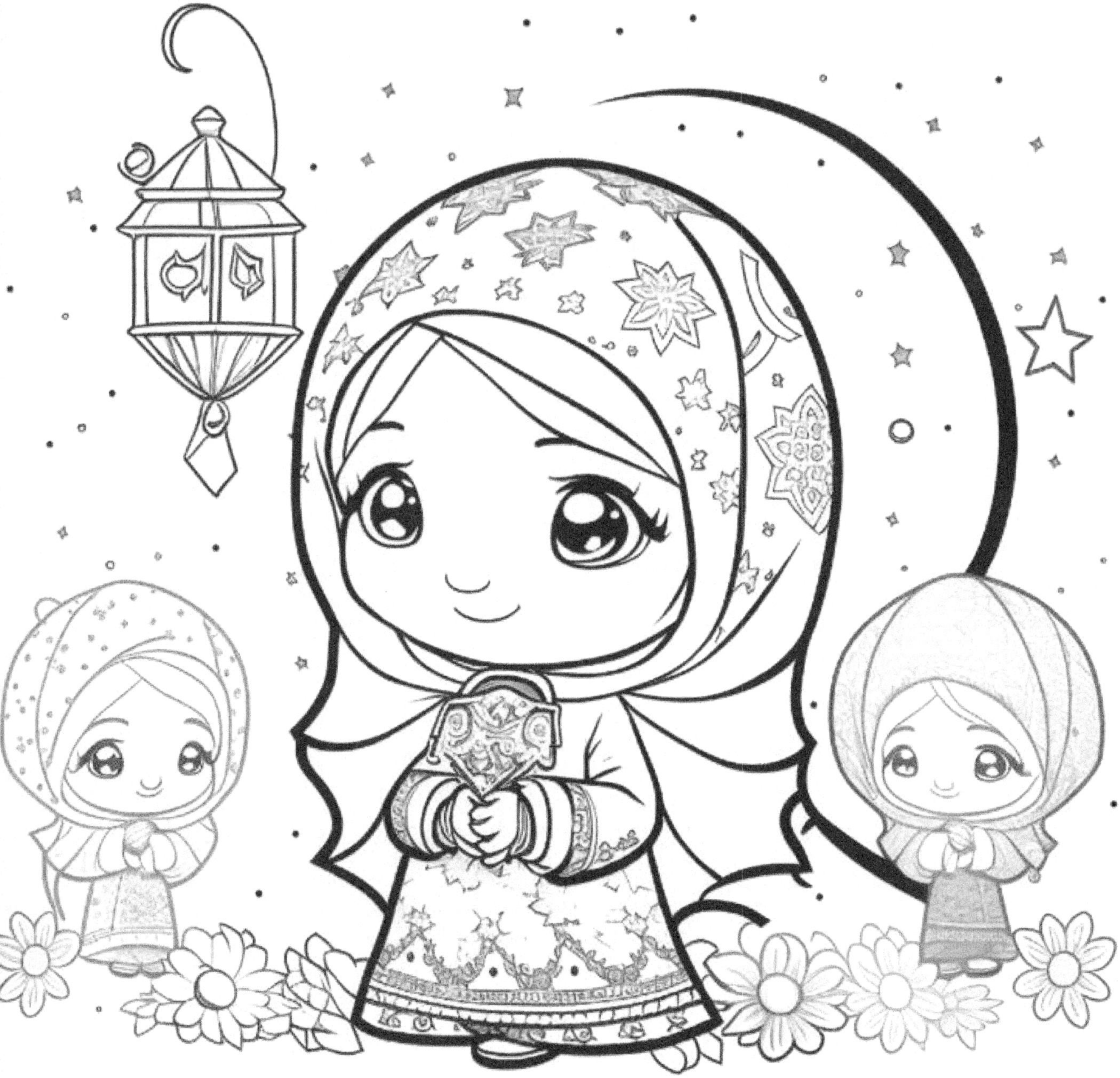

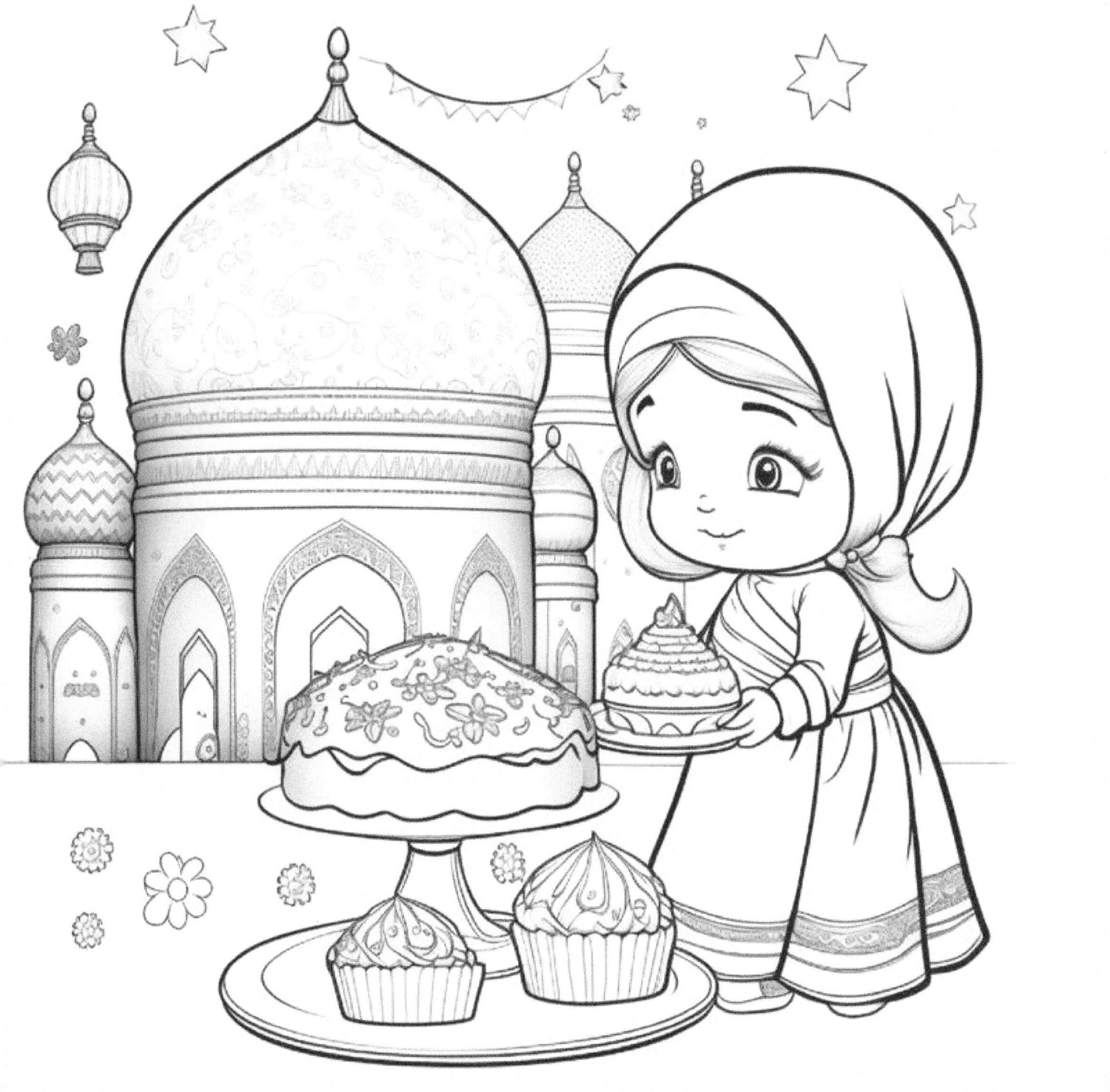

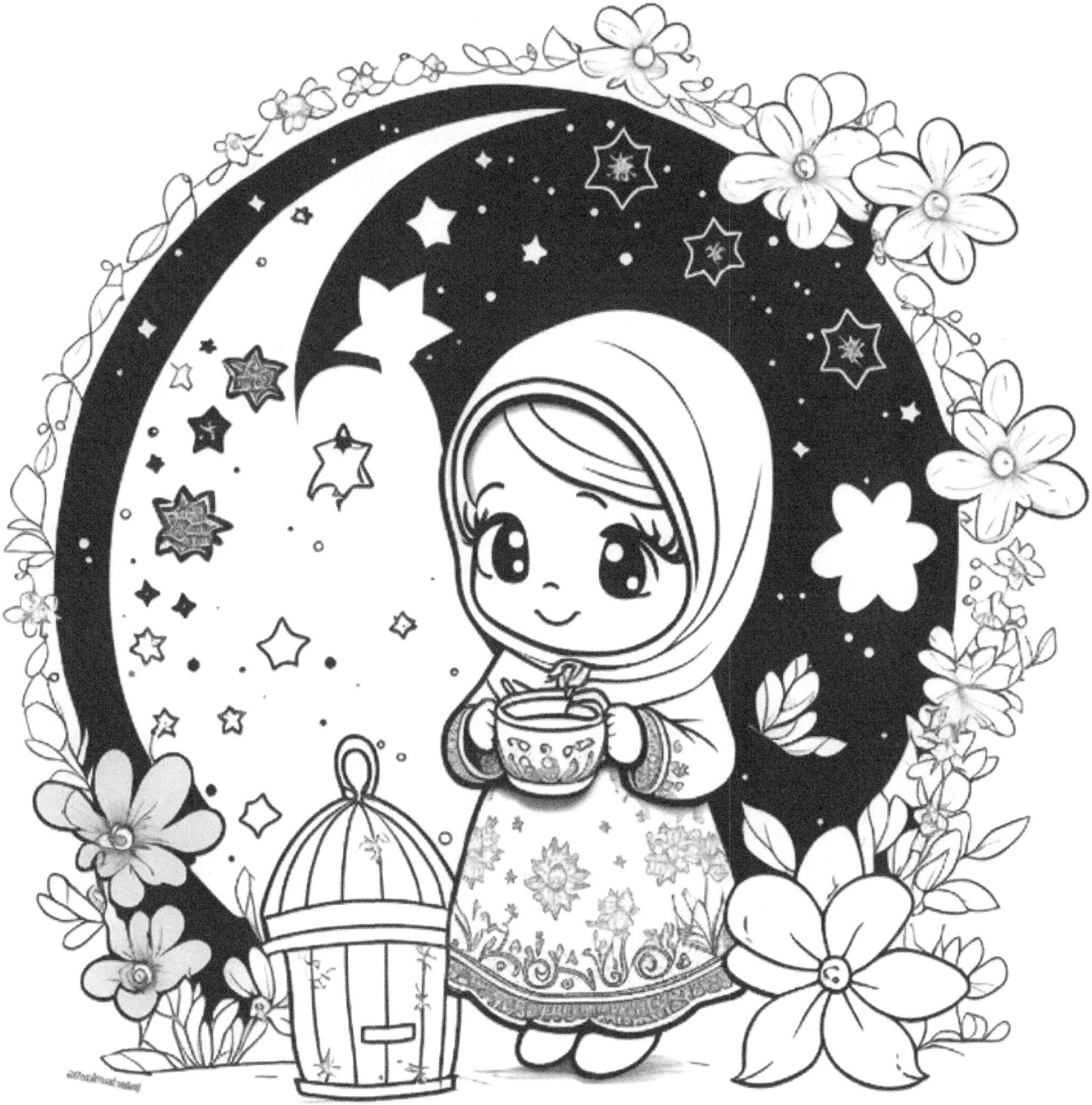

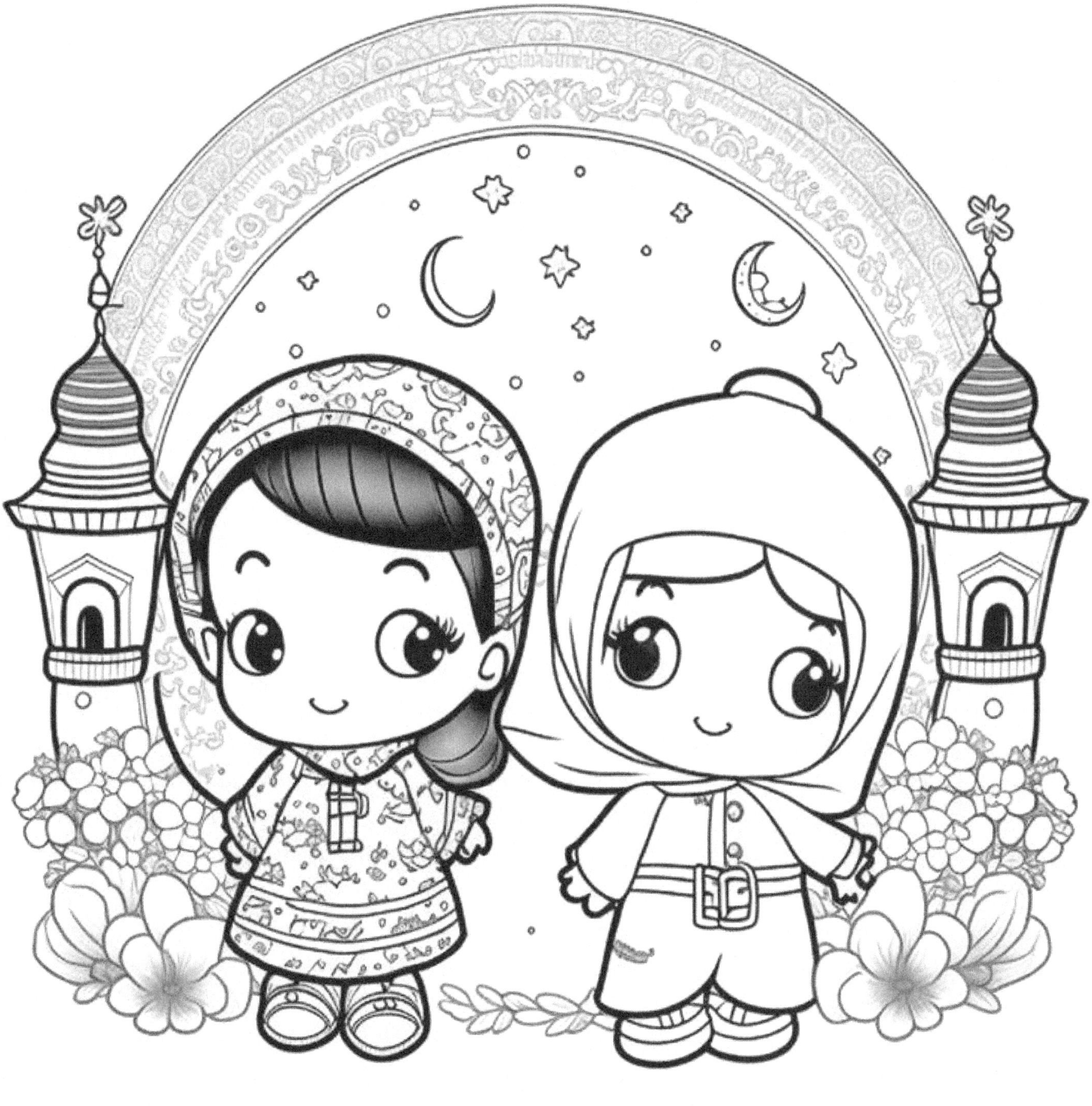

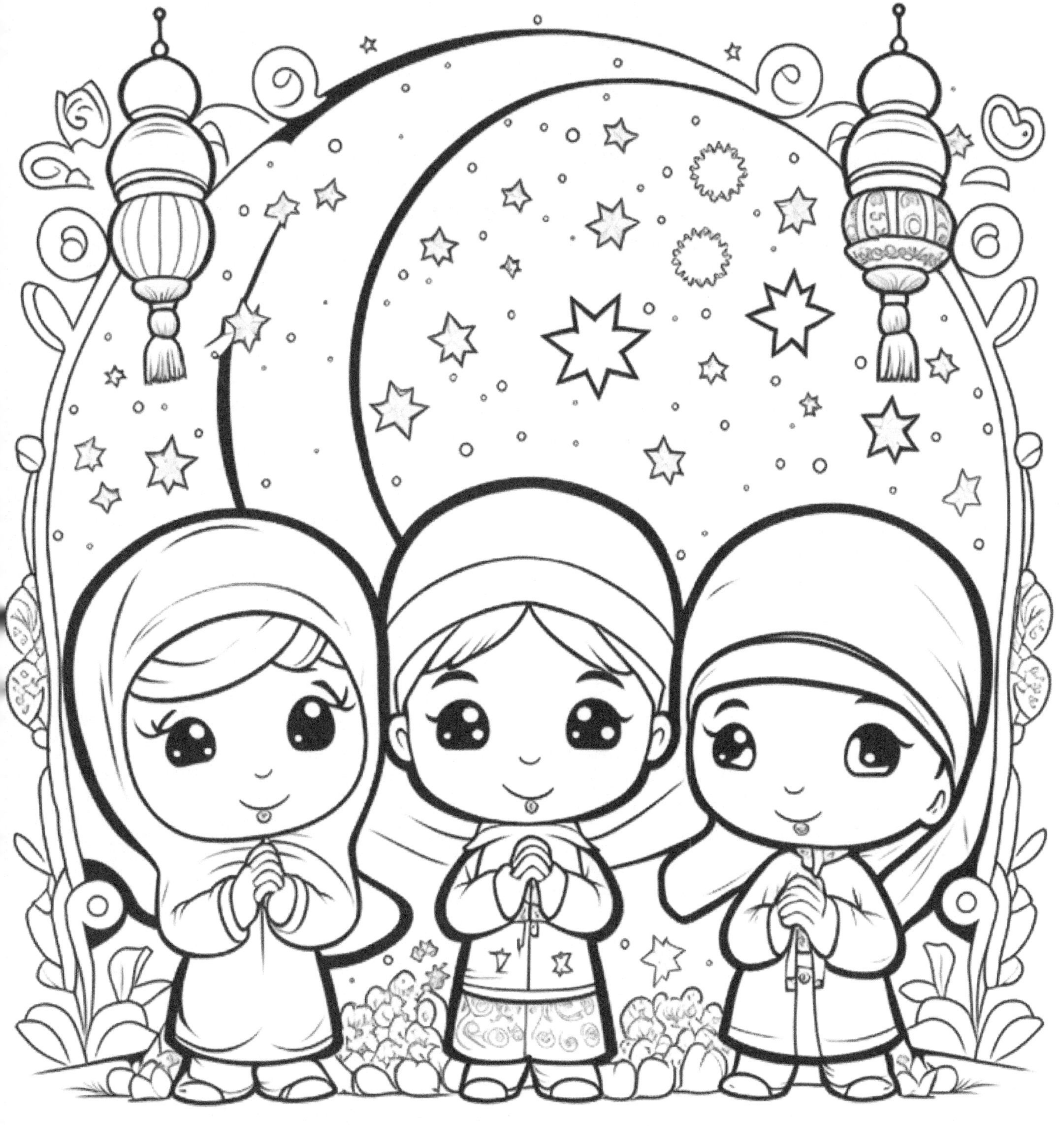

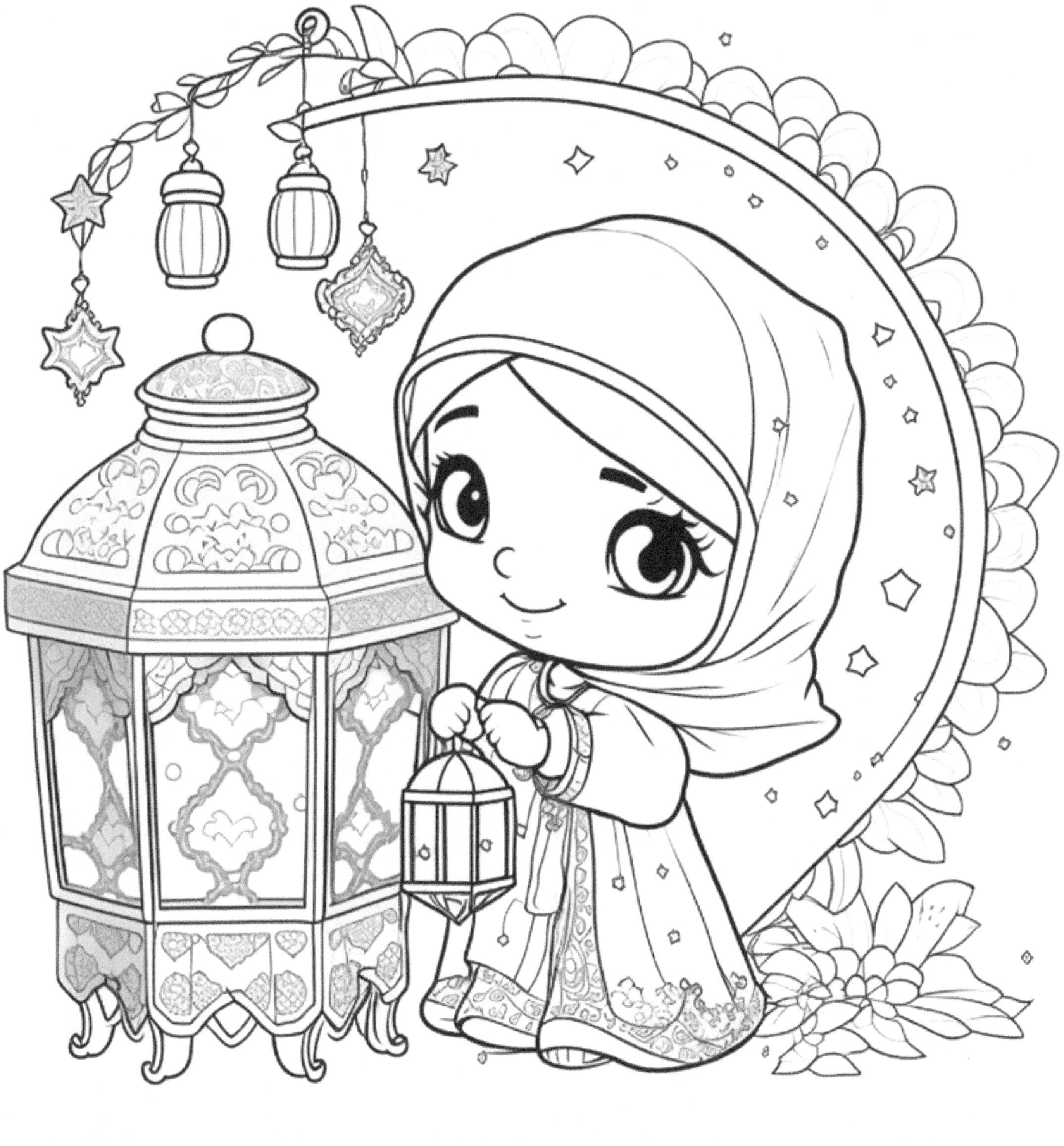

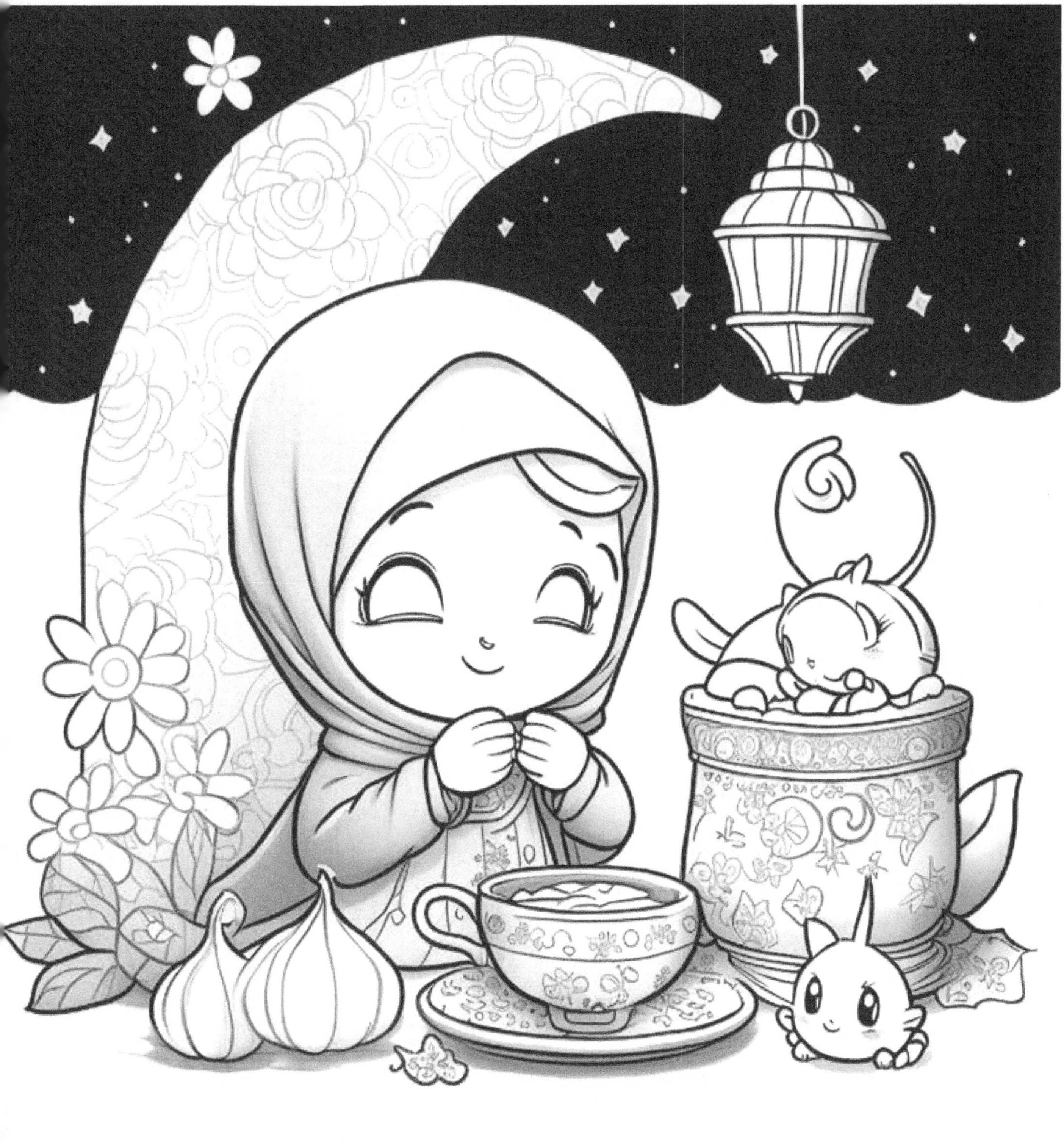

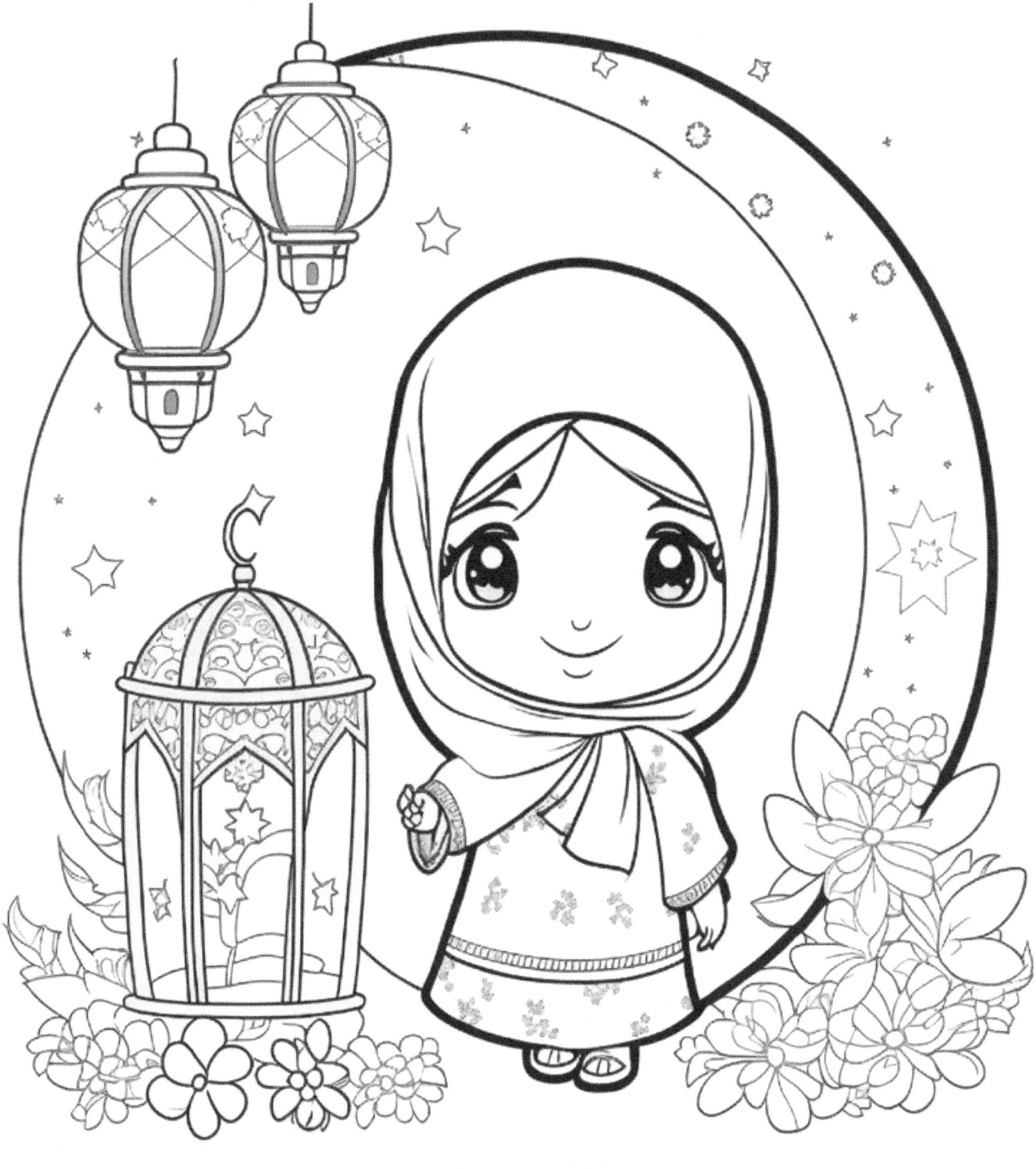

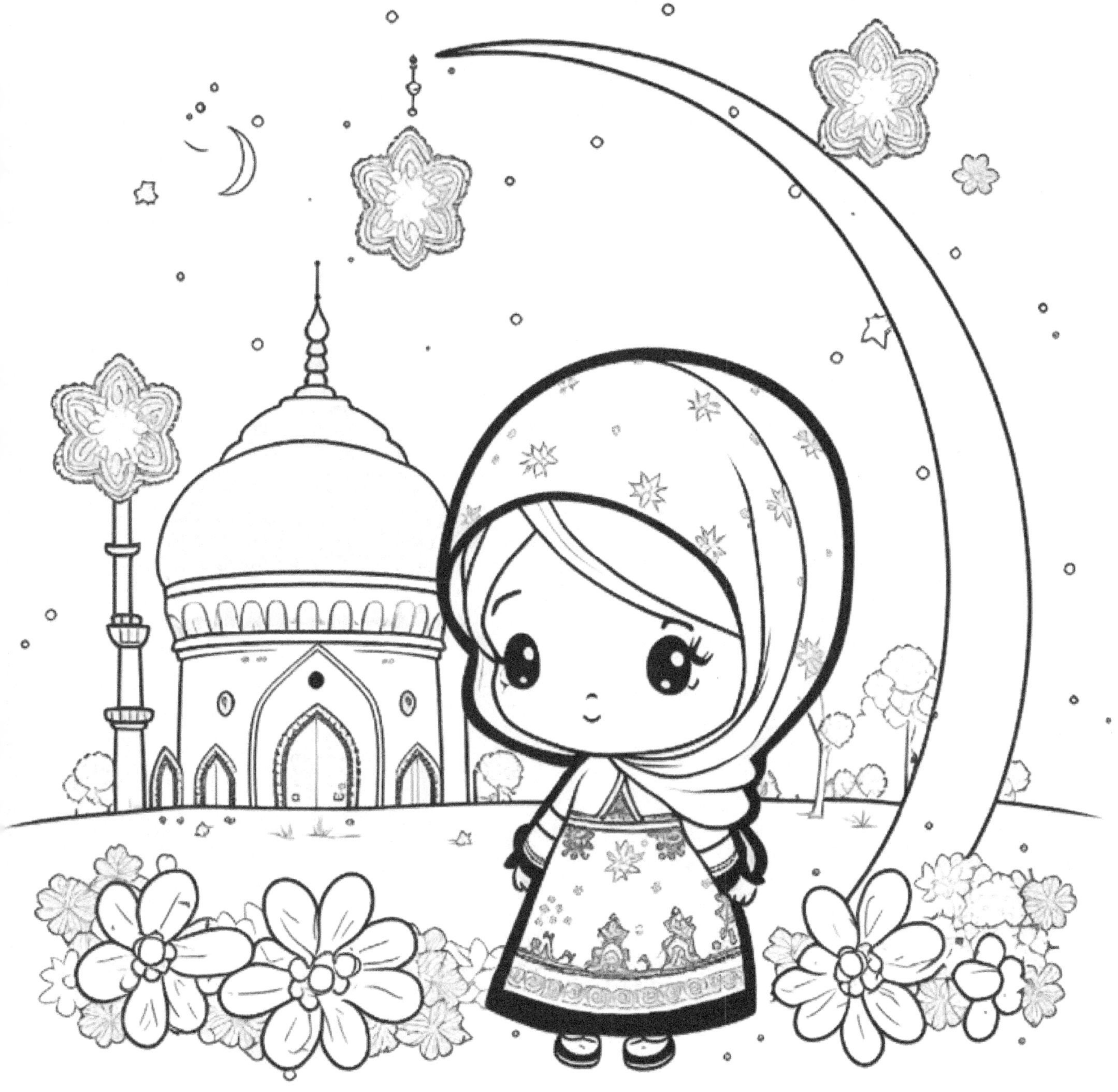

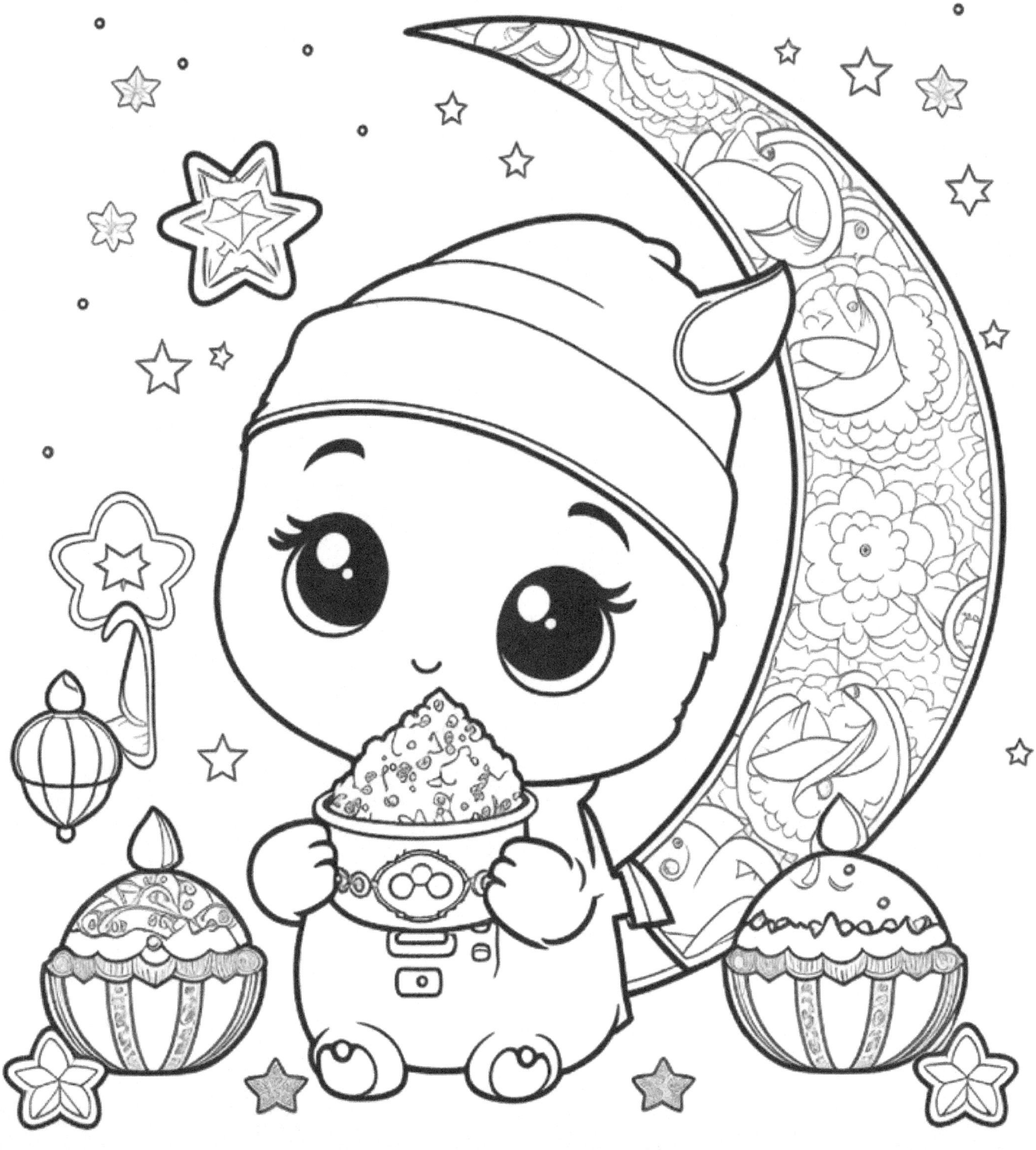

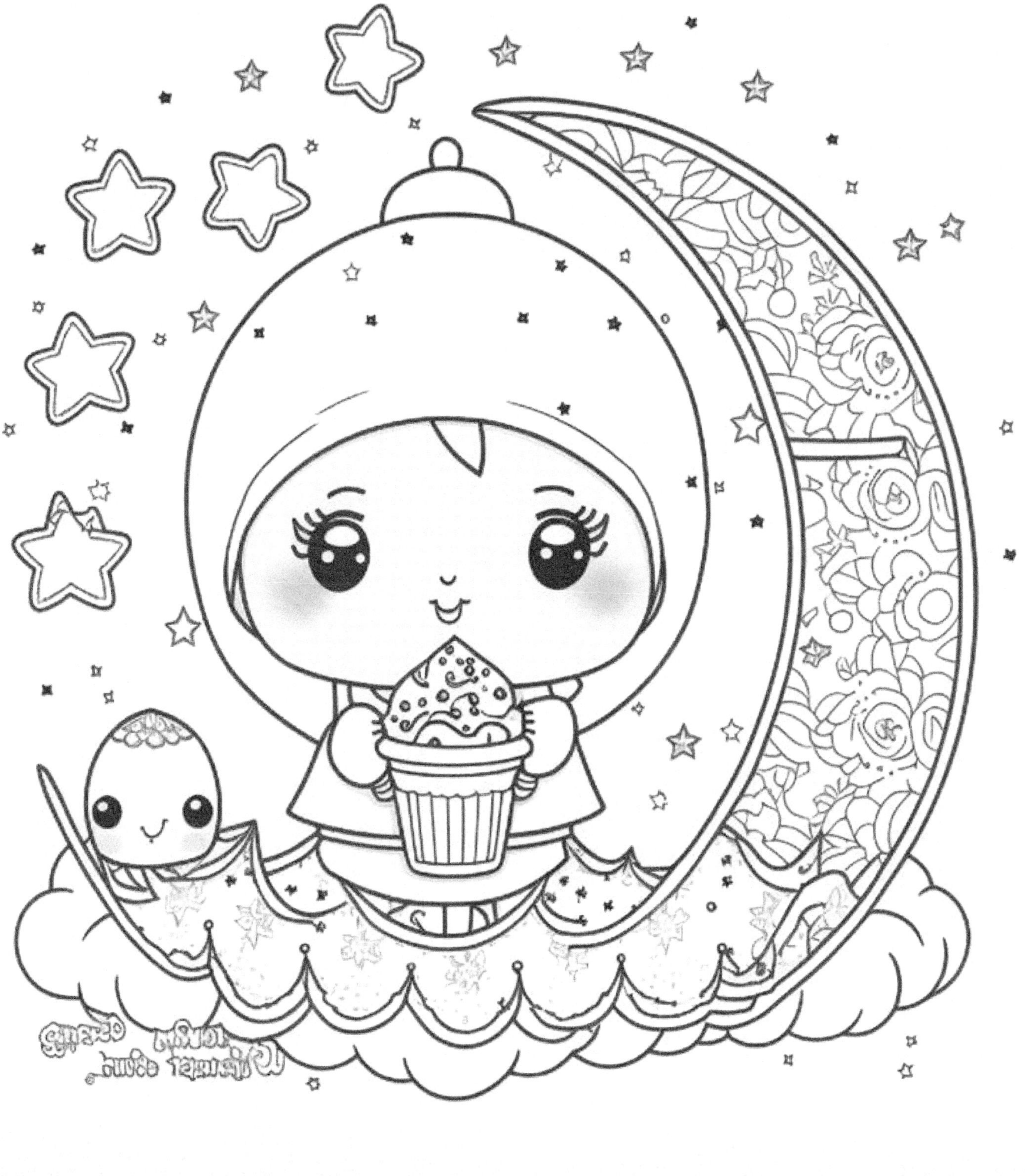

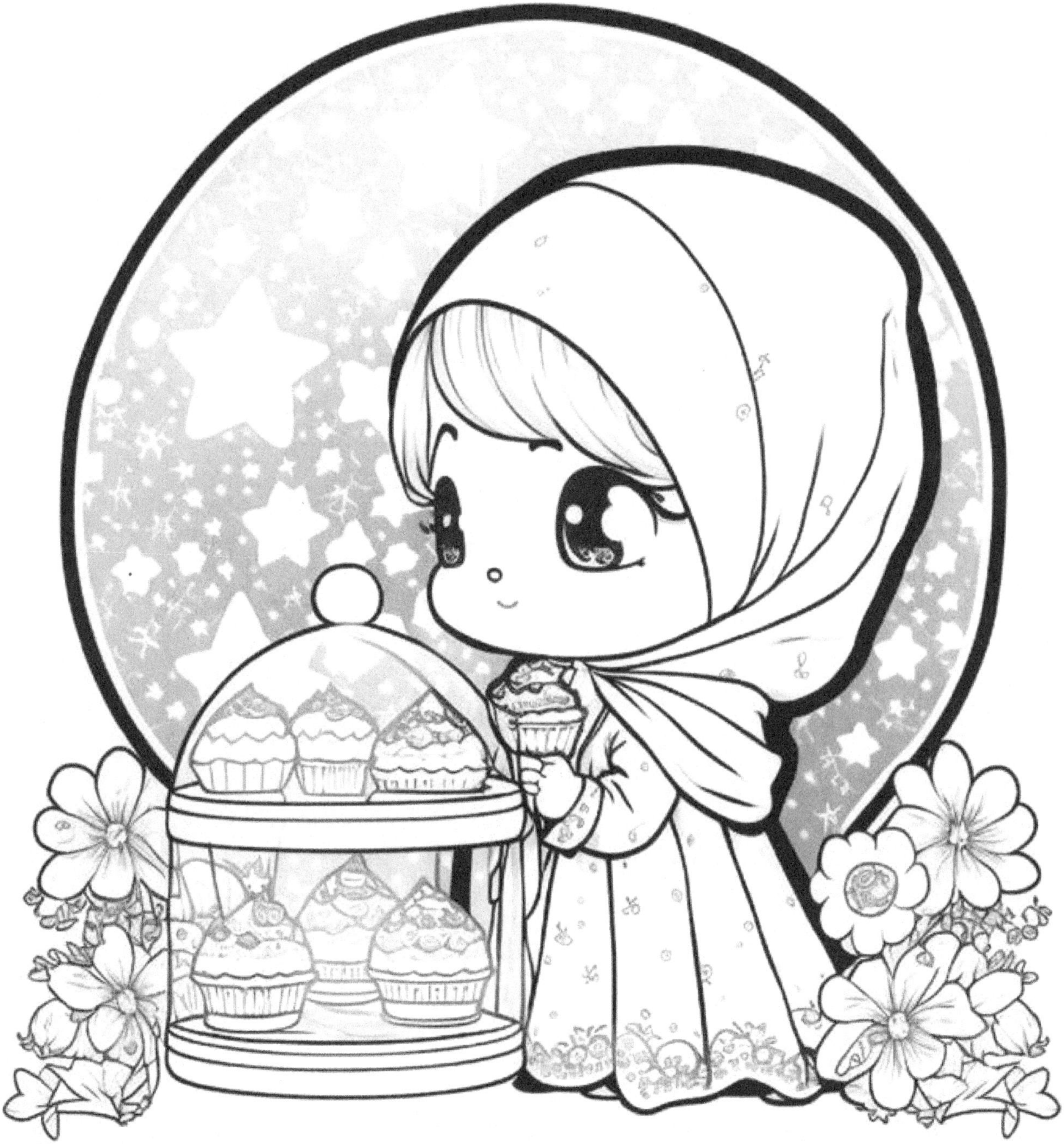

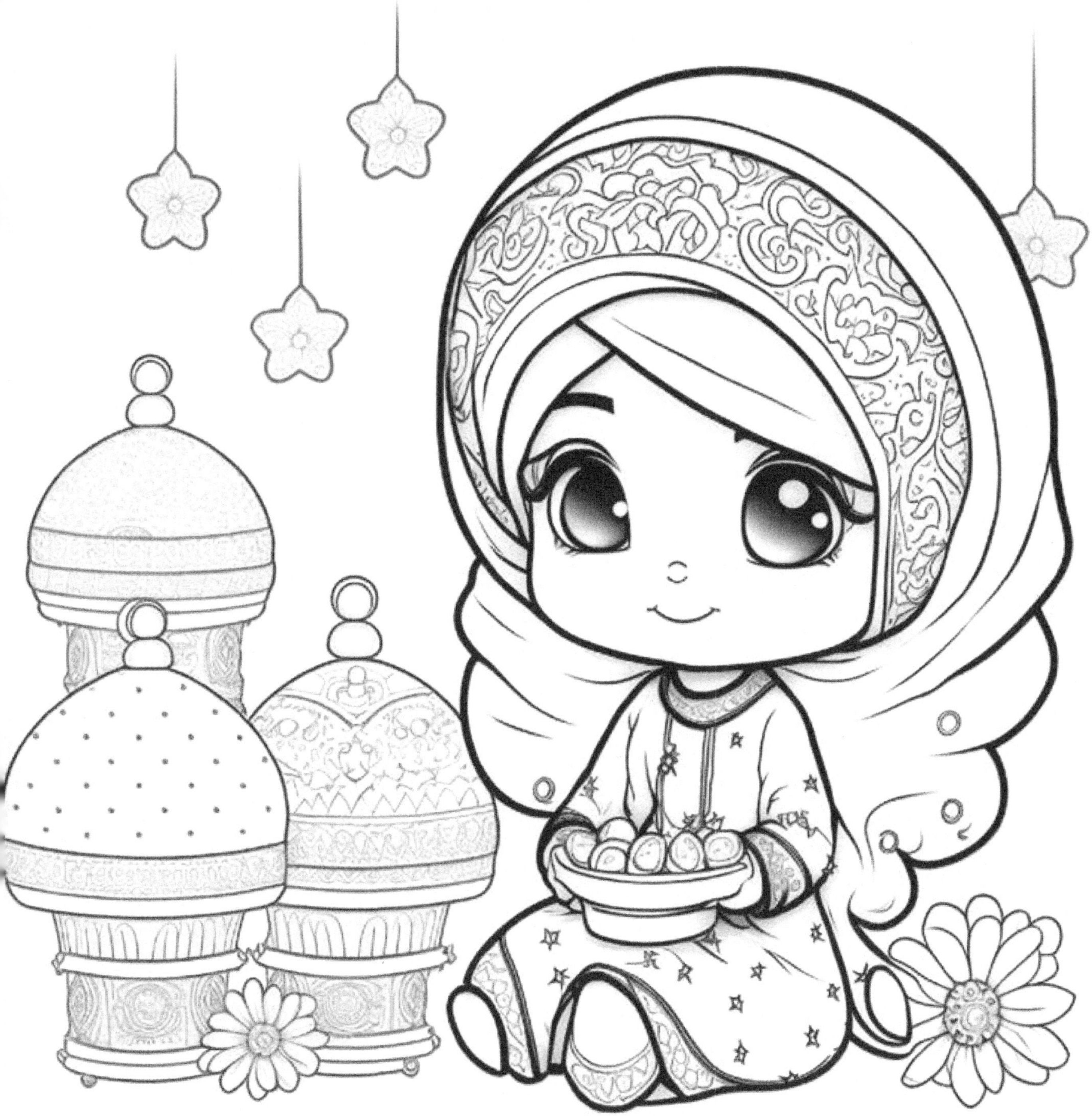

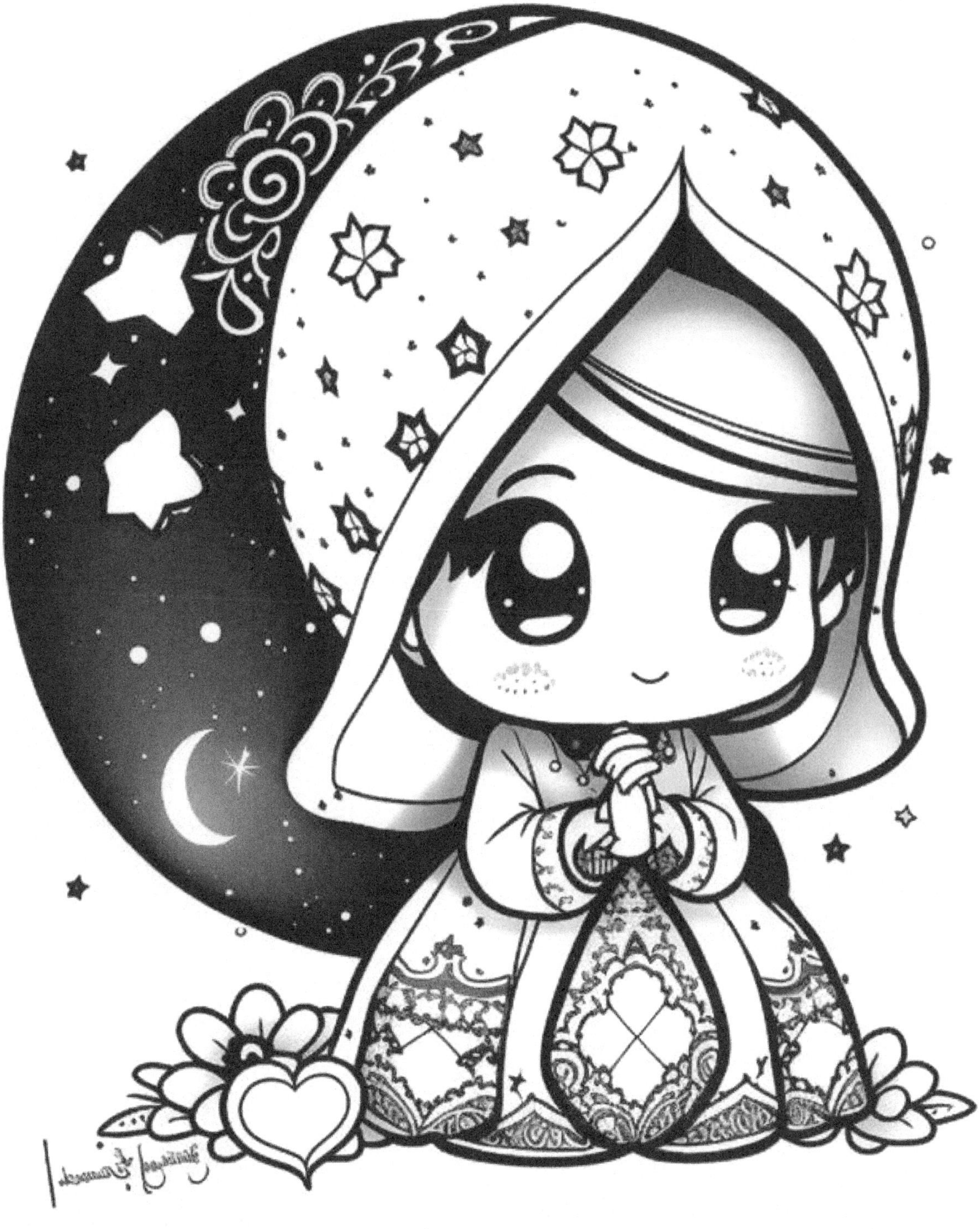

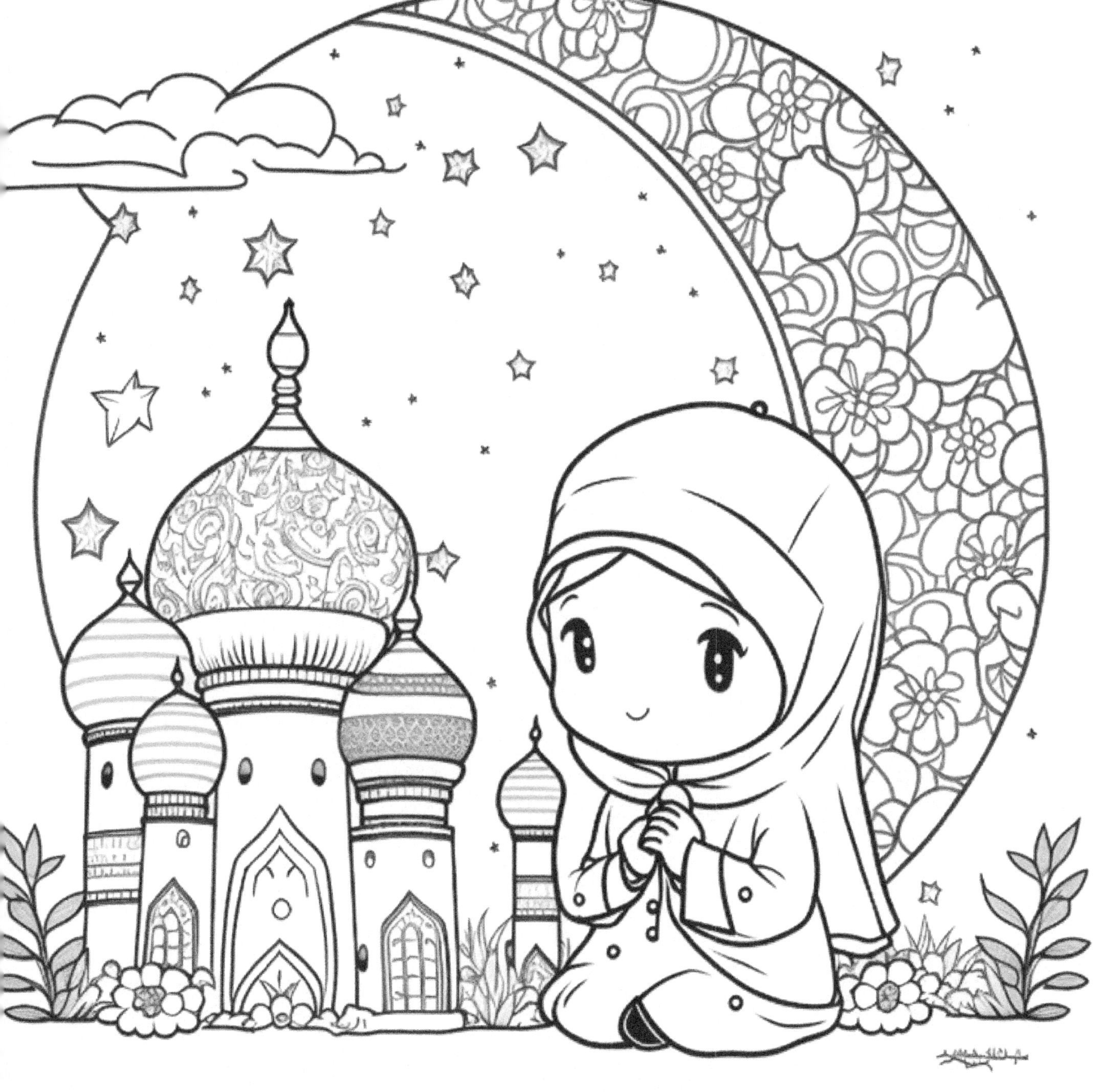

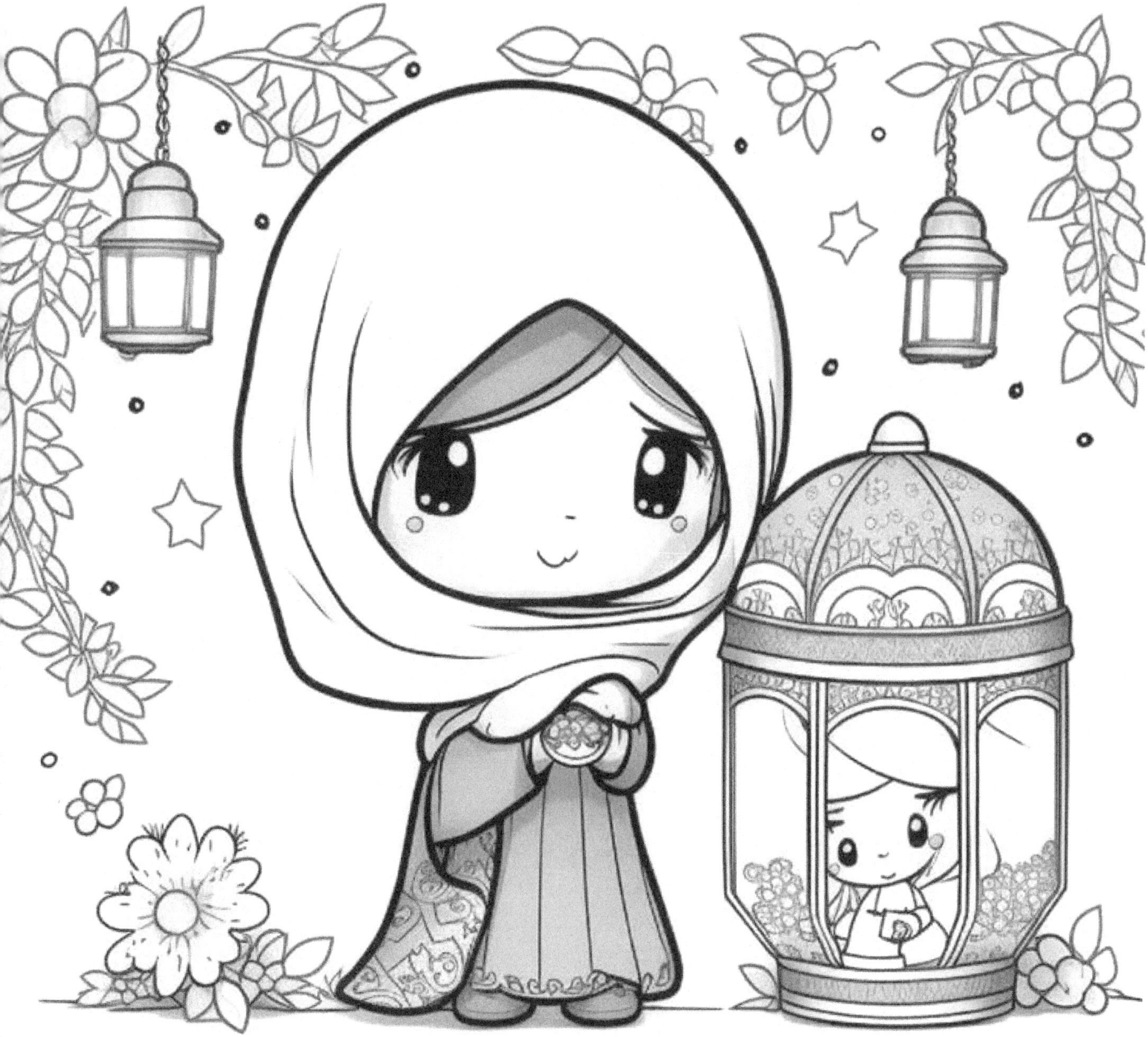

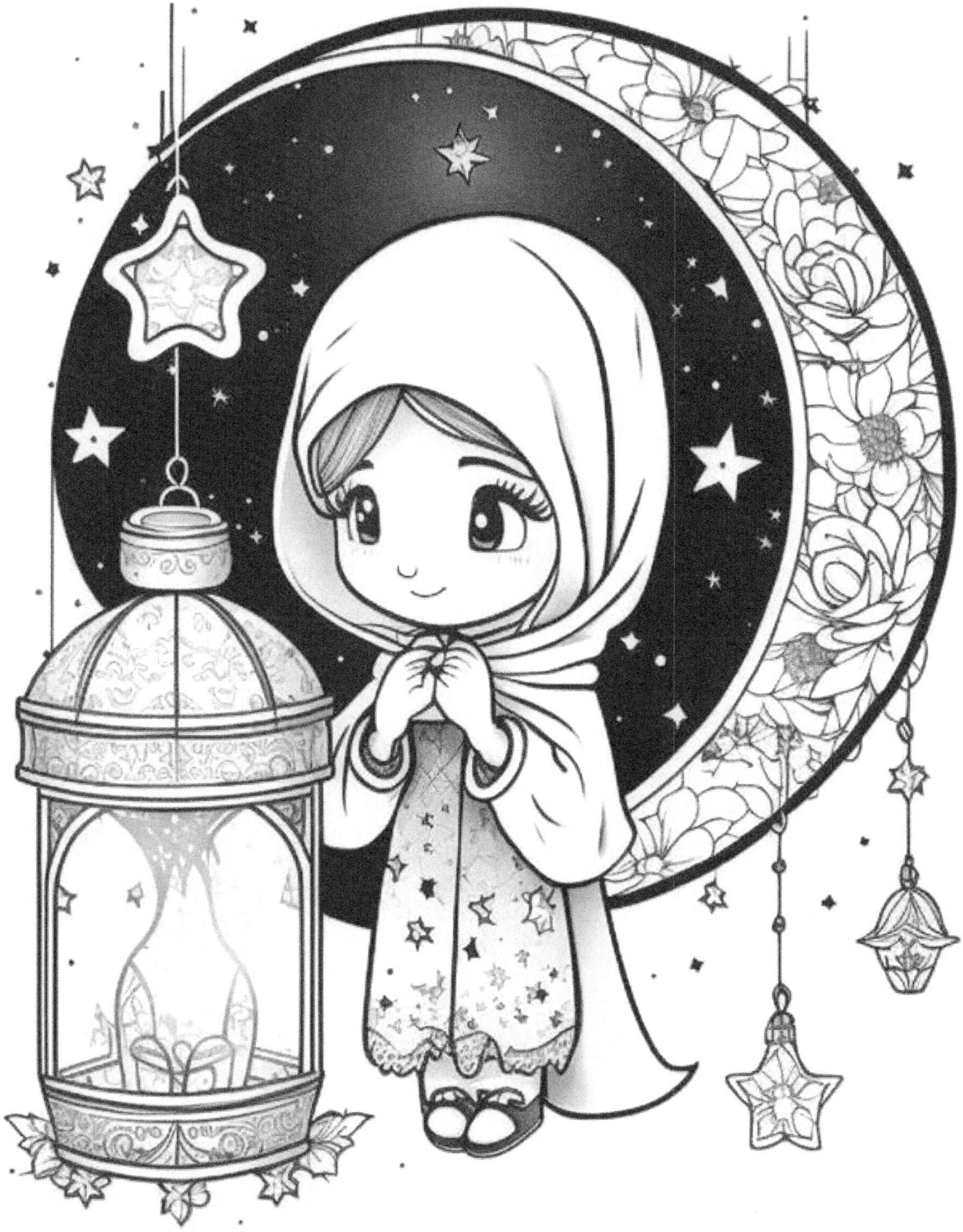

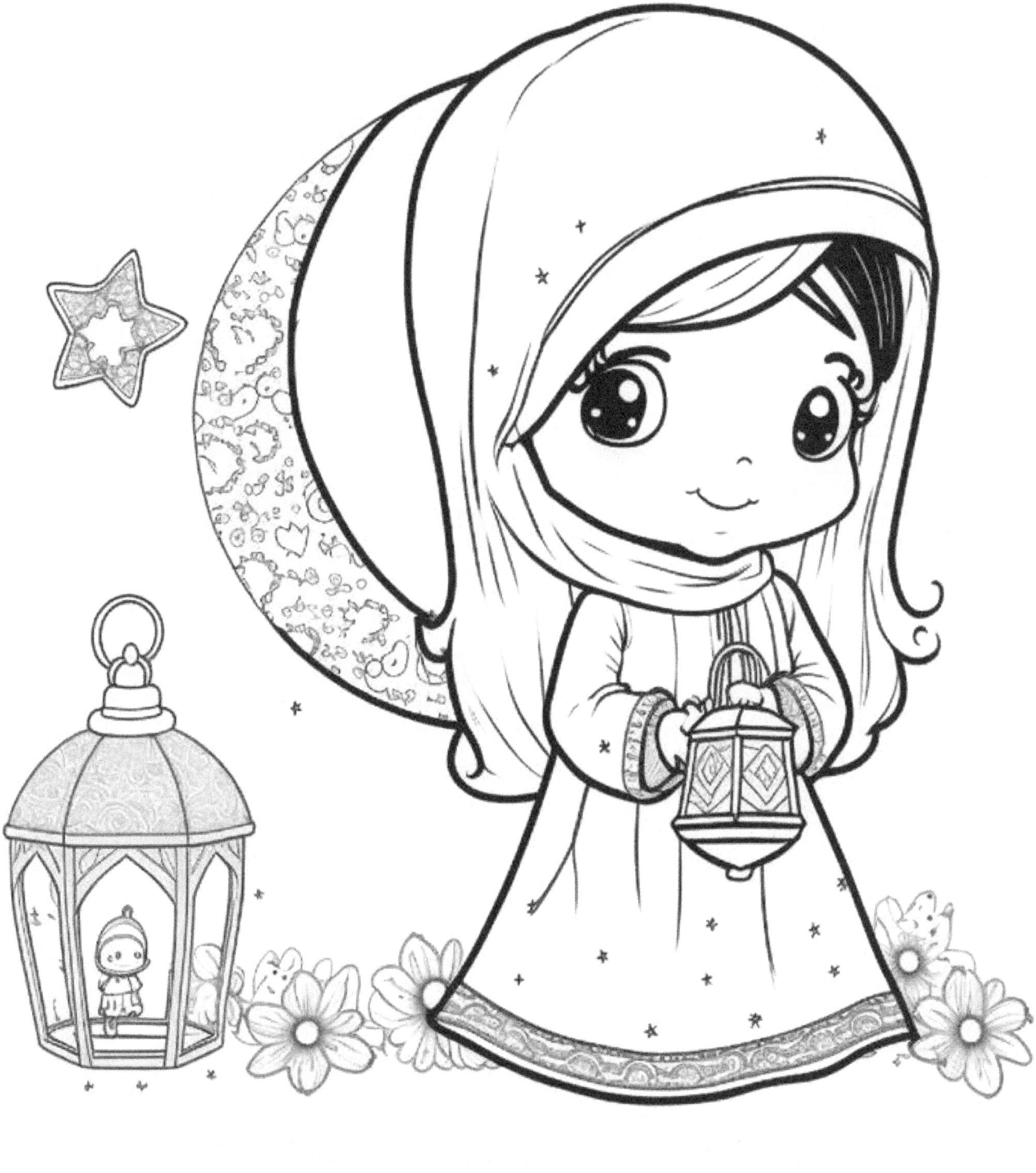

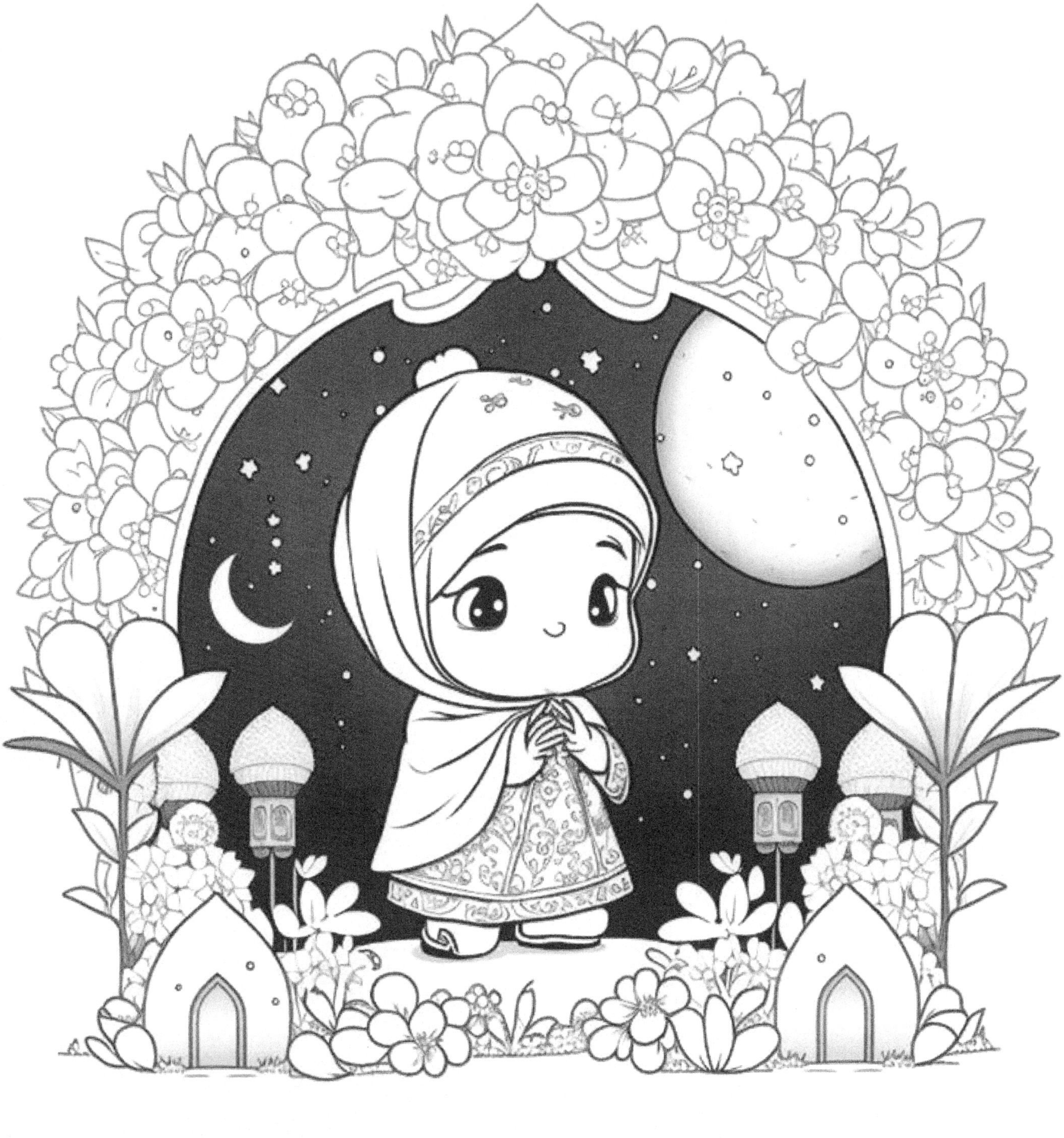

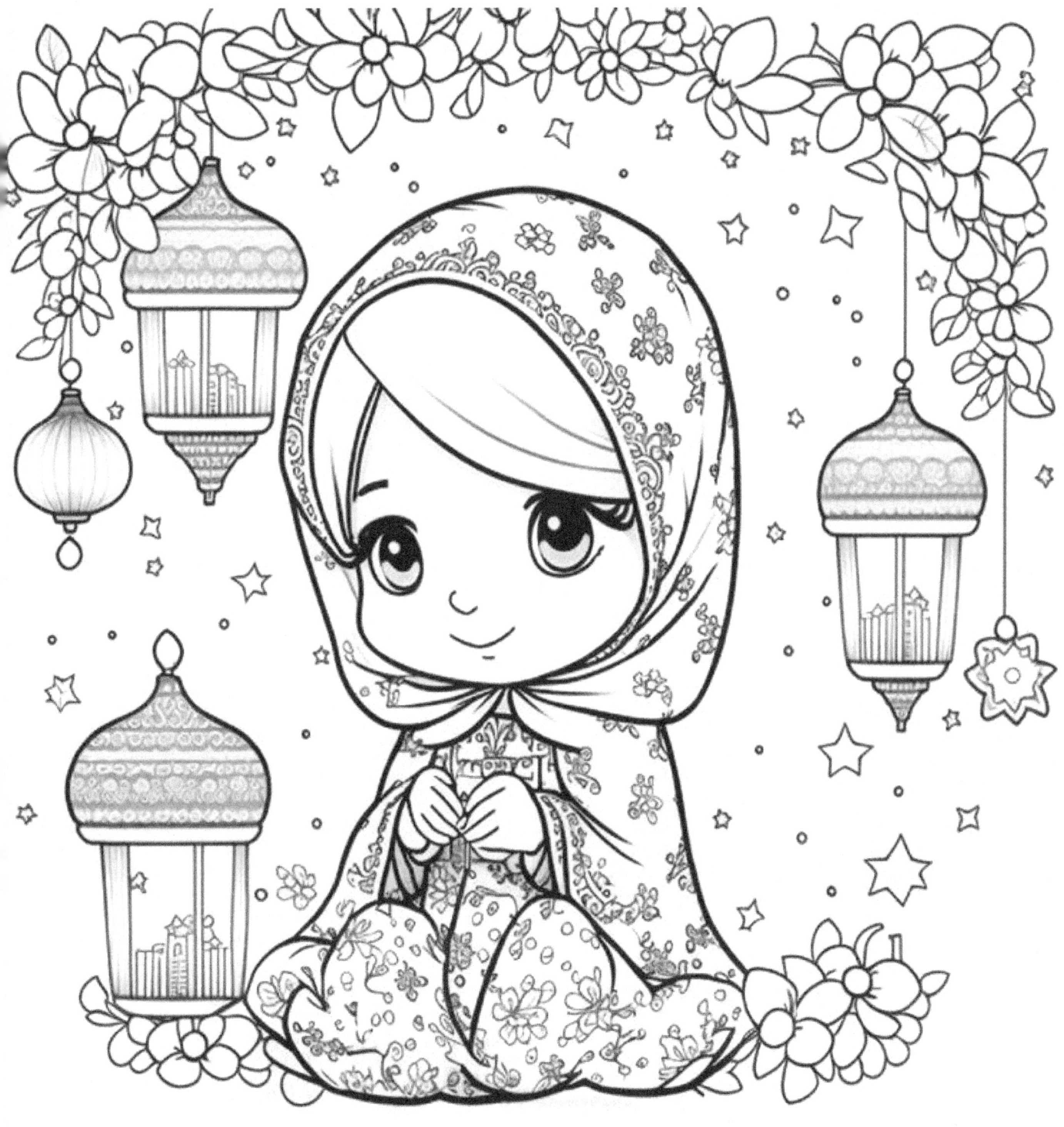

Made in the USA
Las Vegas, NV
28 February 2024

86470861R00033